Presenting:

ORANGE SPORANGE

A REVIEW OF THE ORANGE HUE!

Words & Art by: Brianna Davis

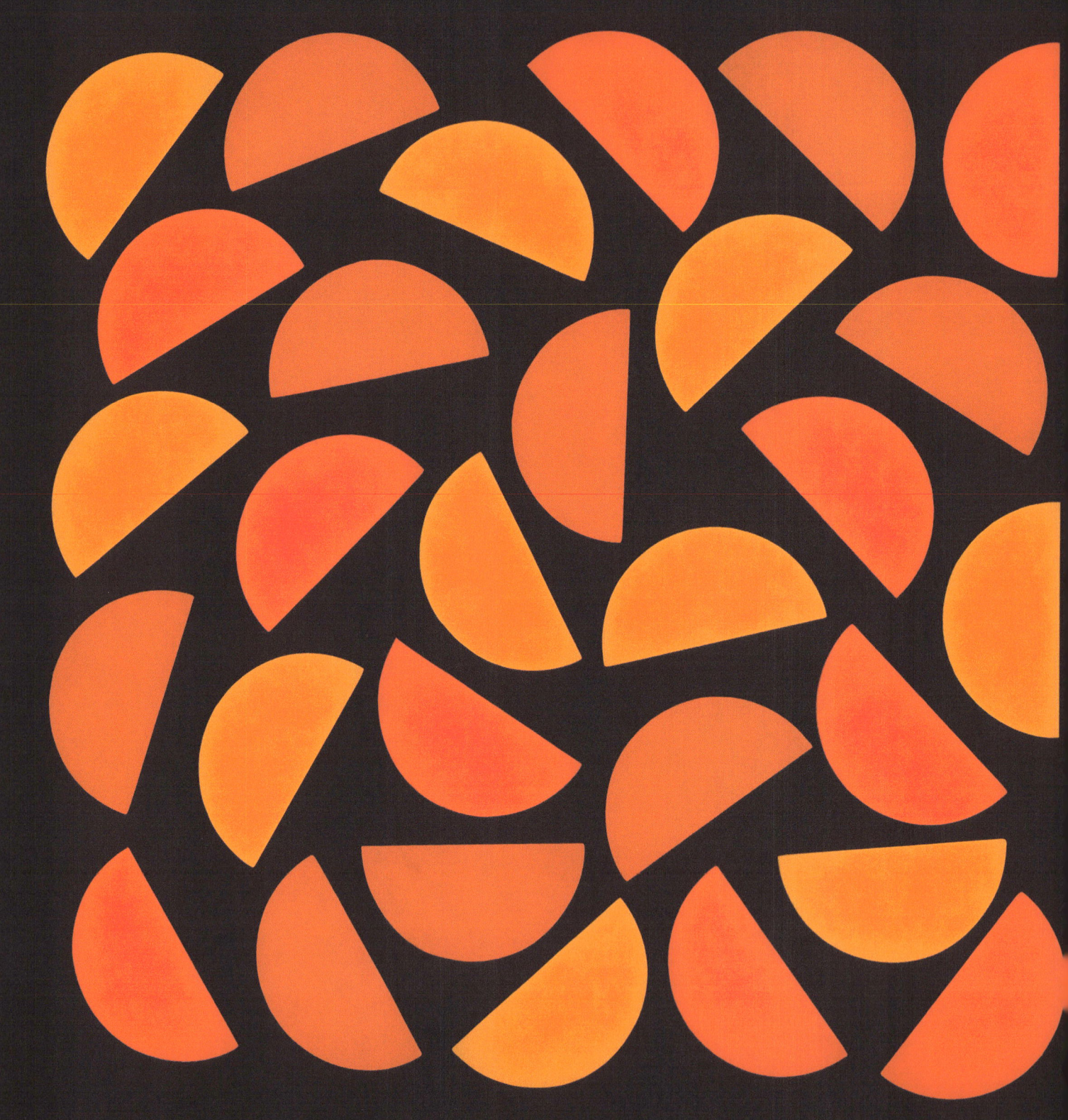

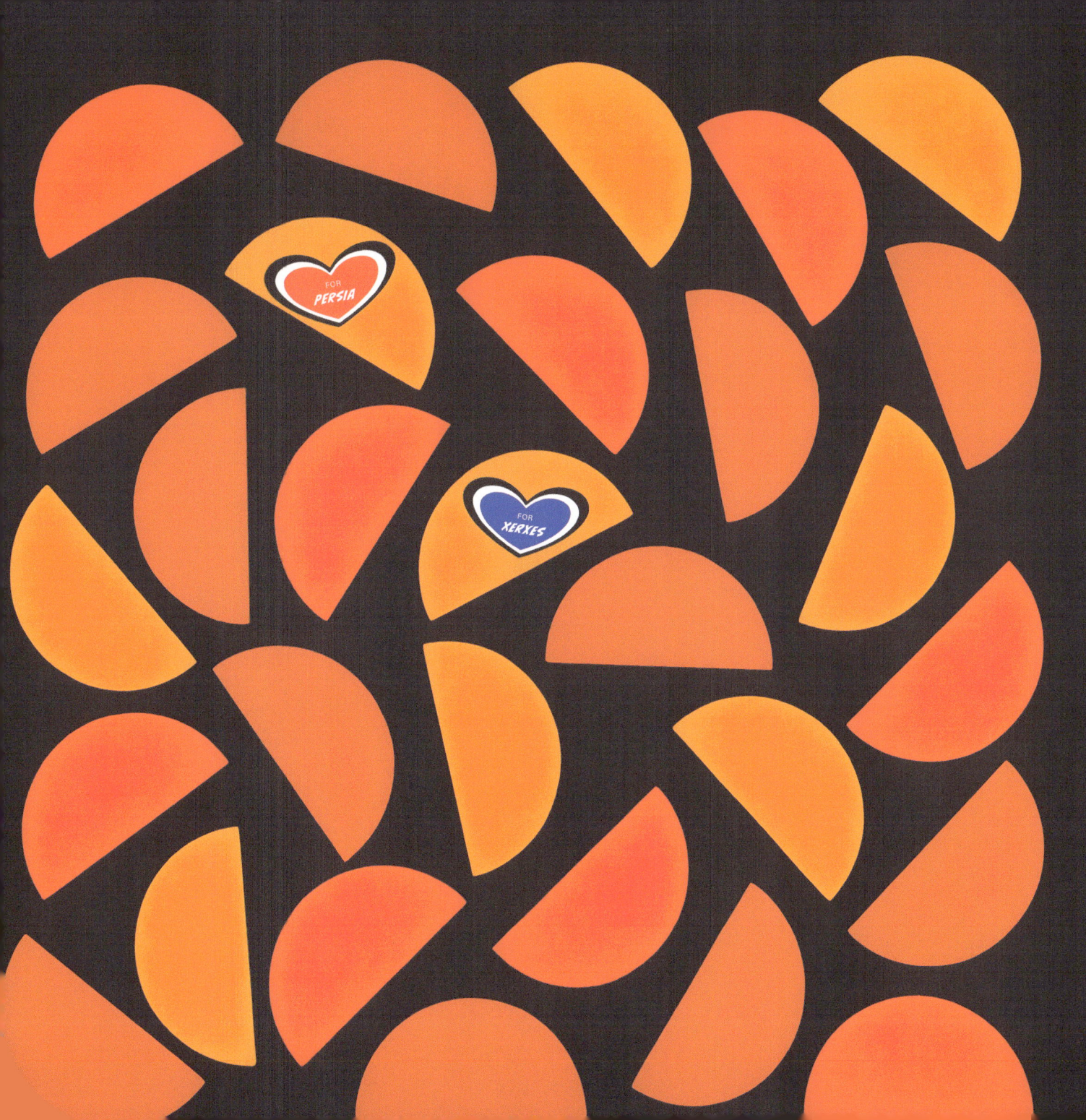

ORANGE

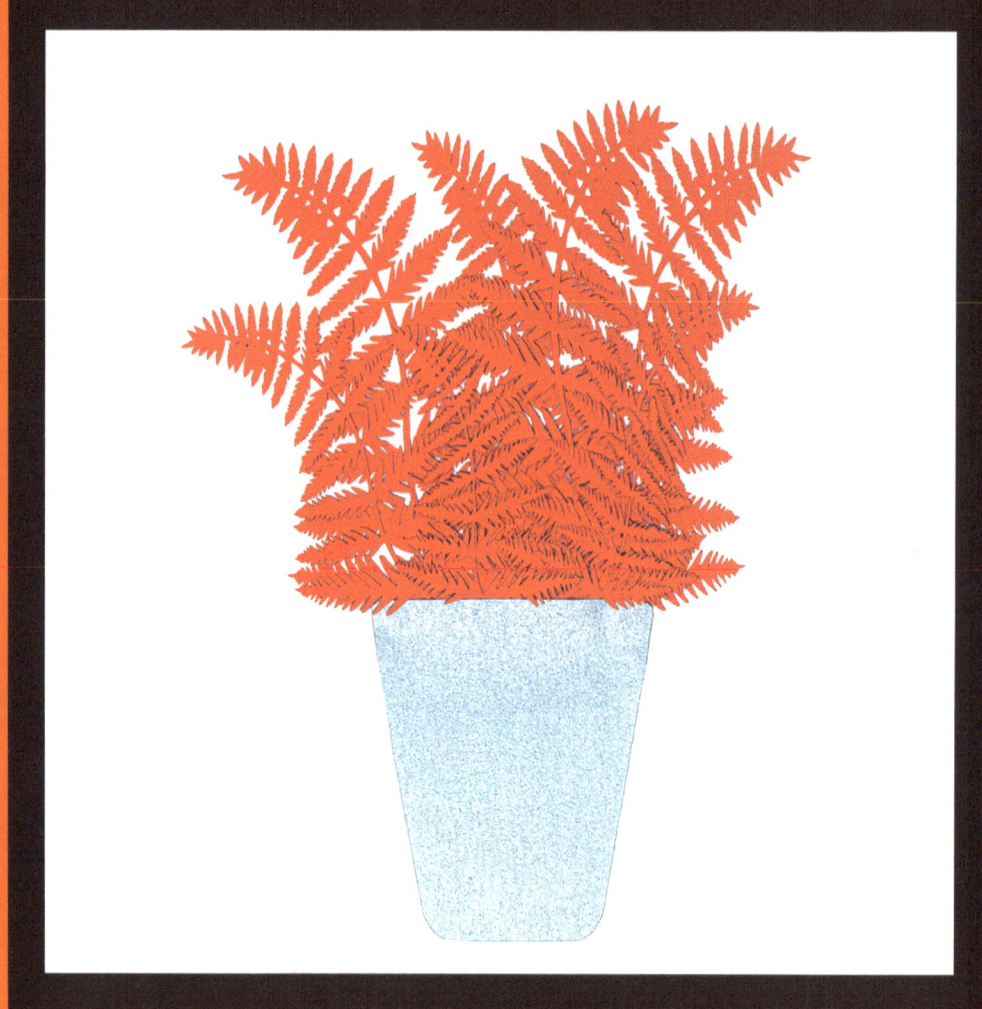

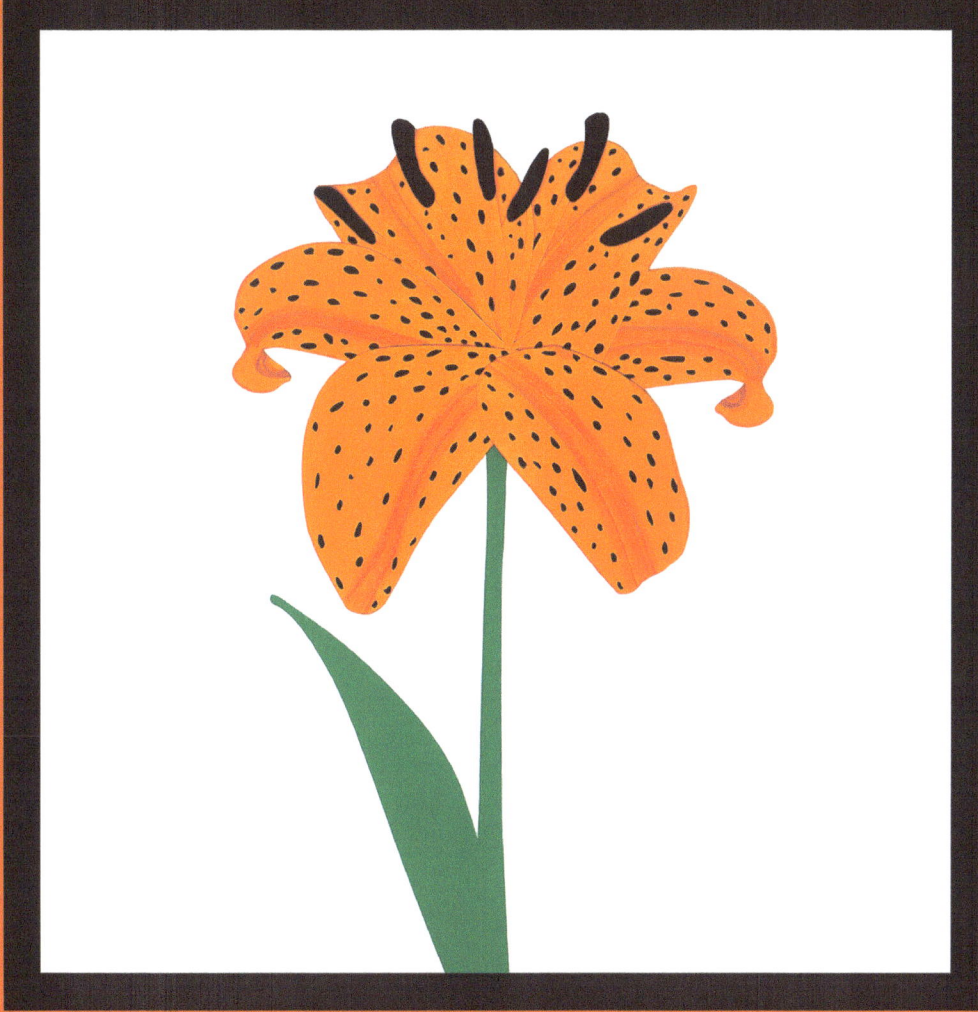

LET'S START WITH THIS TIGER LILY; ISN'T IT PRETTY?

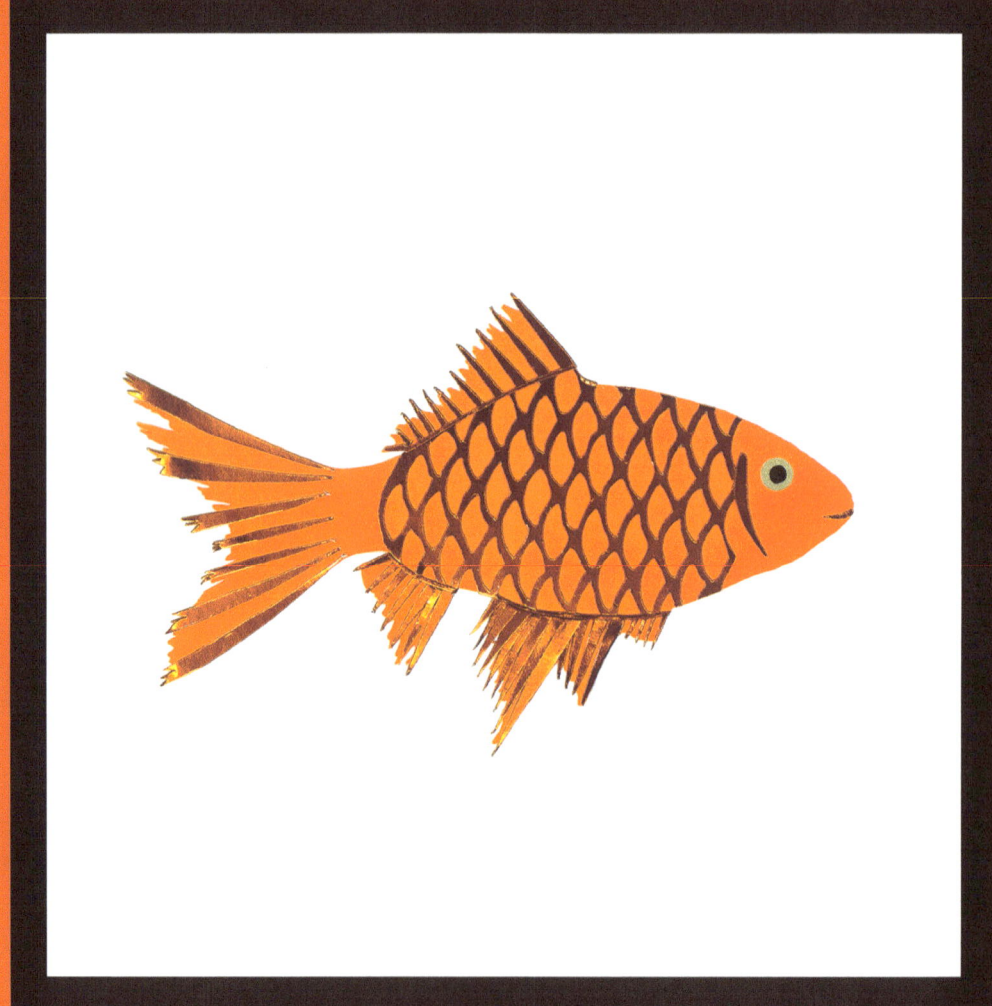

IT IS OUR WISH TO NEXT SHOW YOU THIS GOLDFISH!

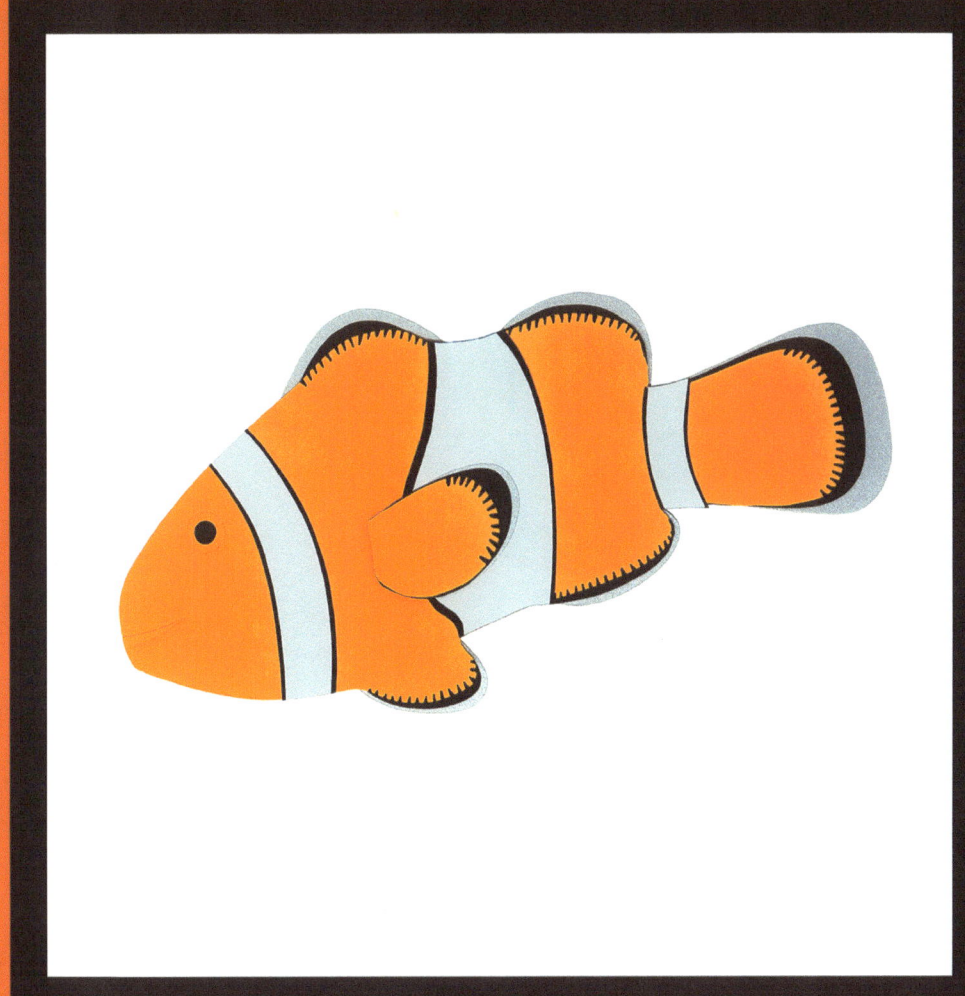

SWISH SWISH, HERE COMES A CLOWNFISH!

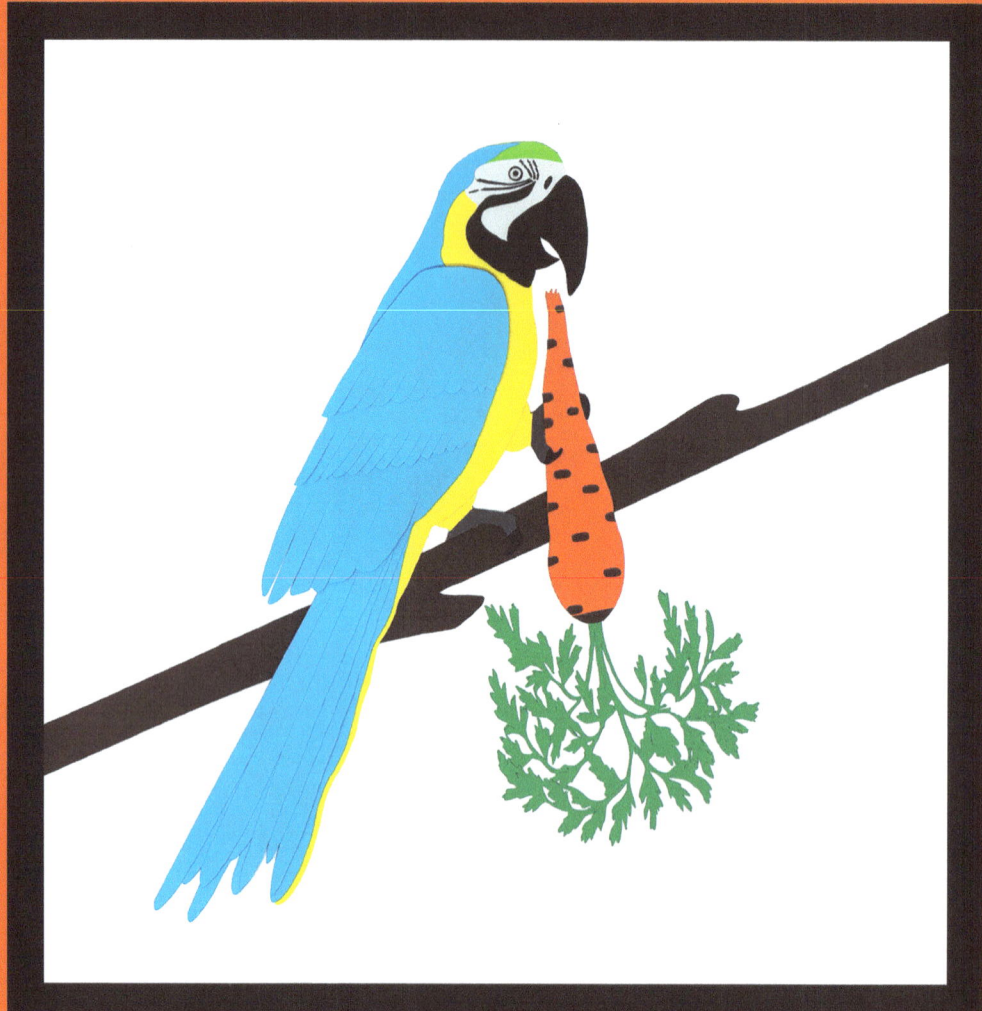

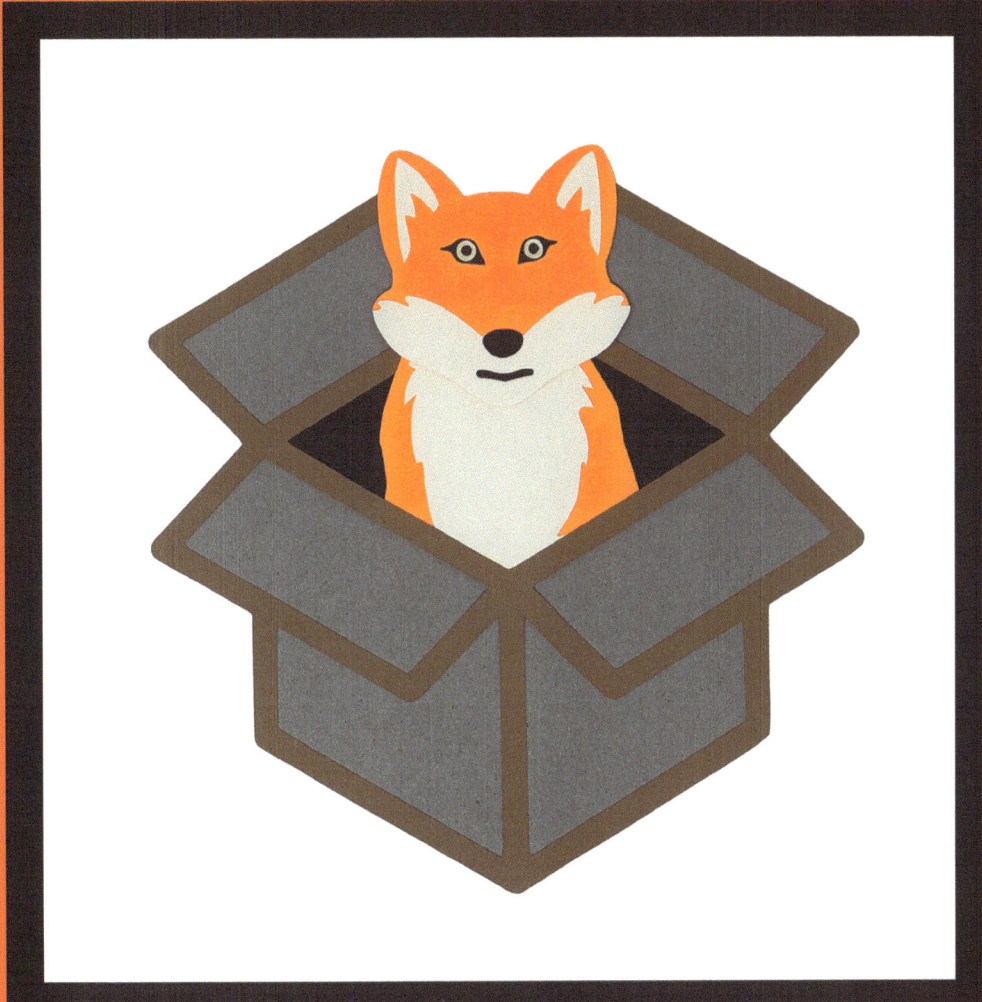

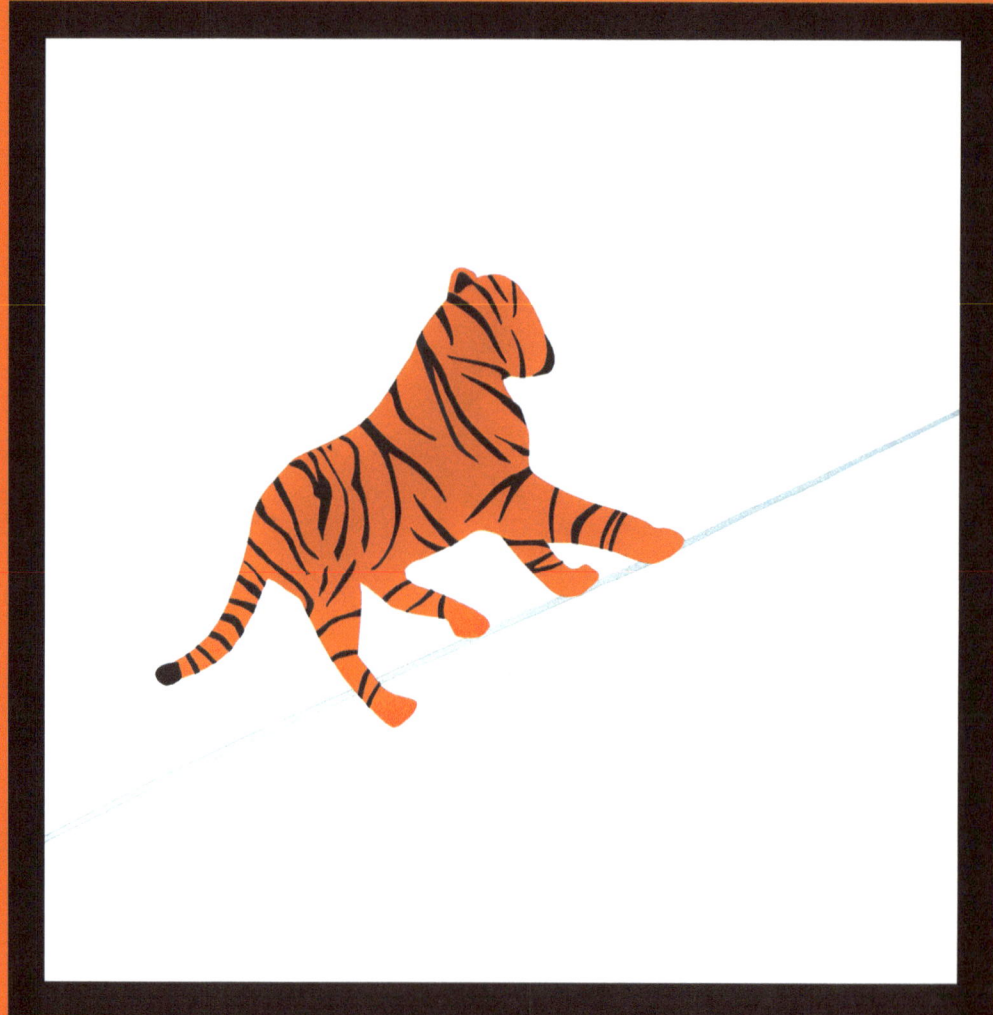

A TIGER ON A WIRE...

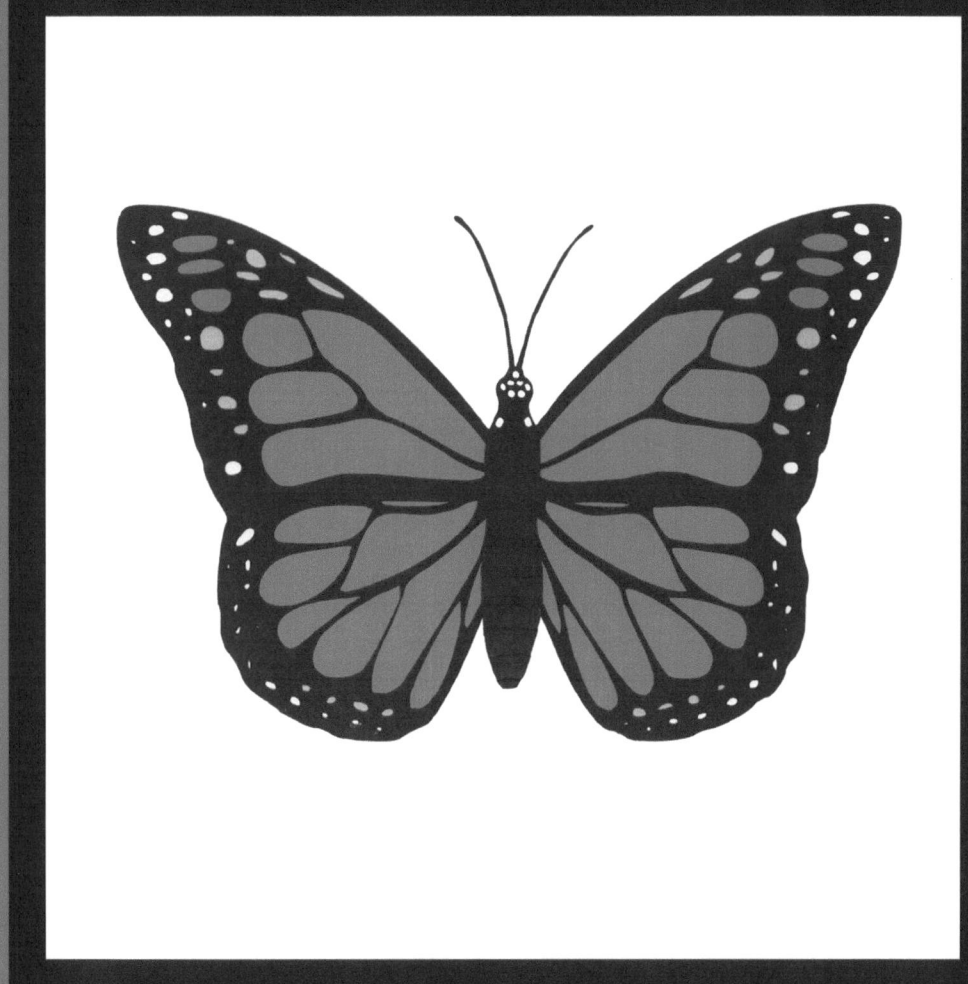

A DARK MONARCH...

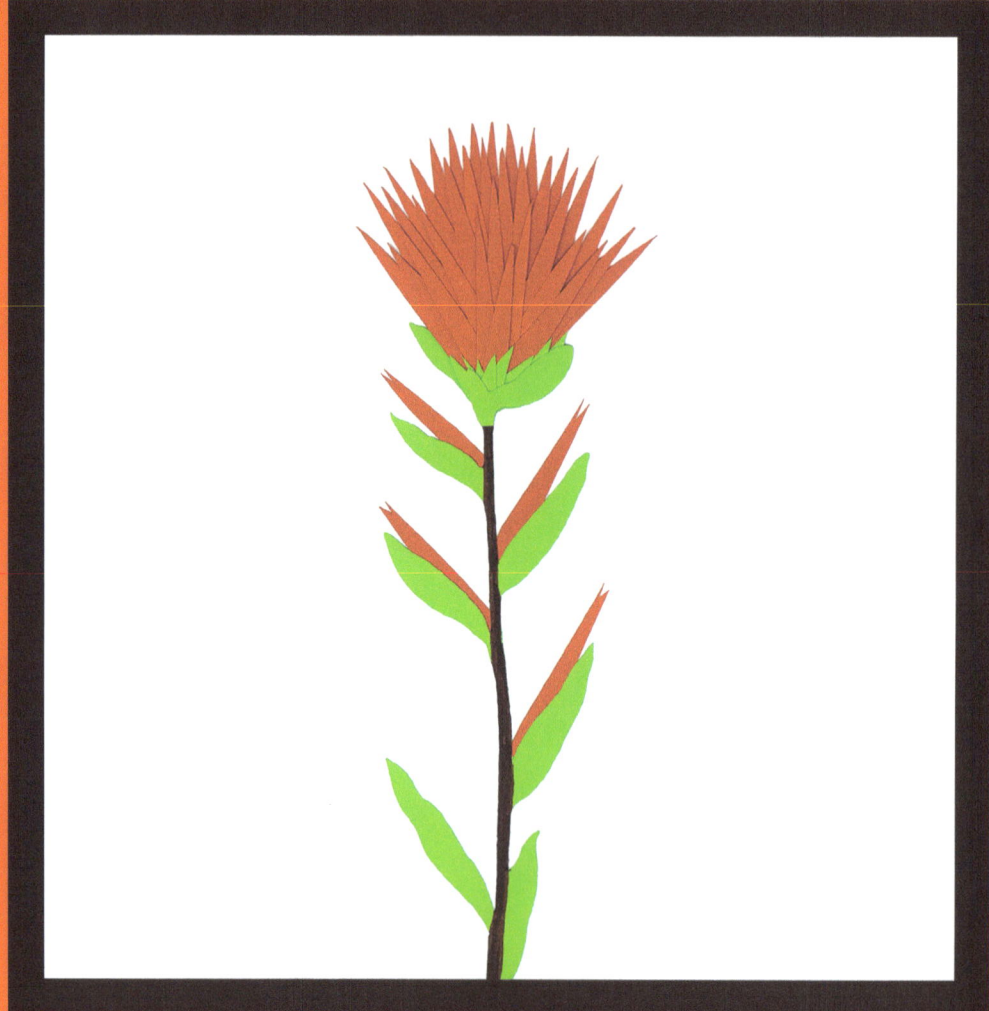

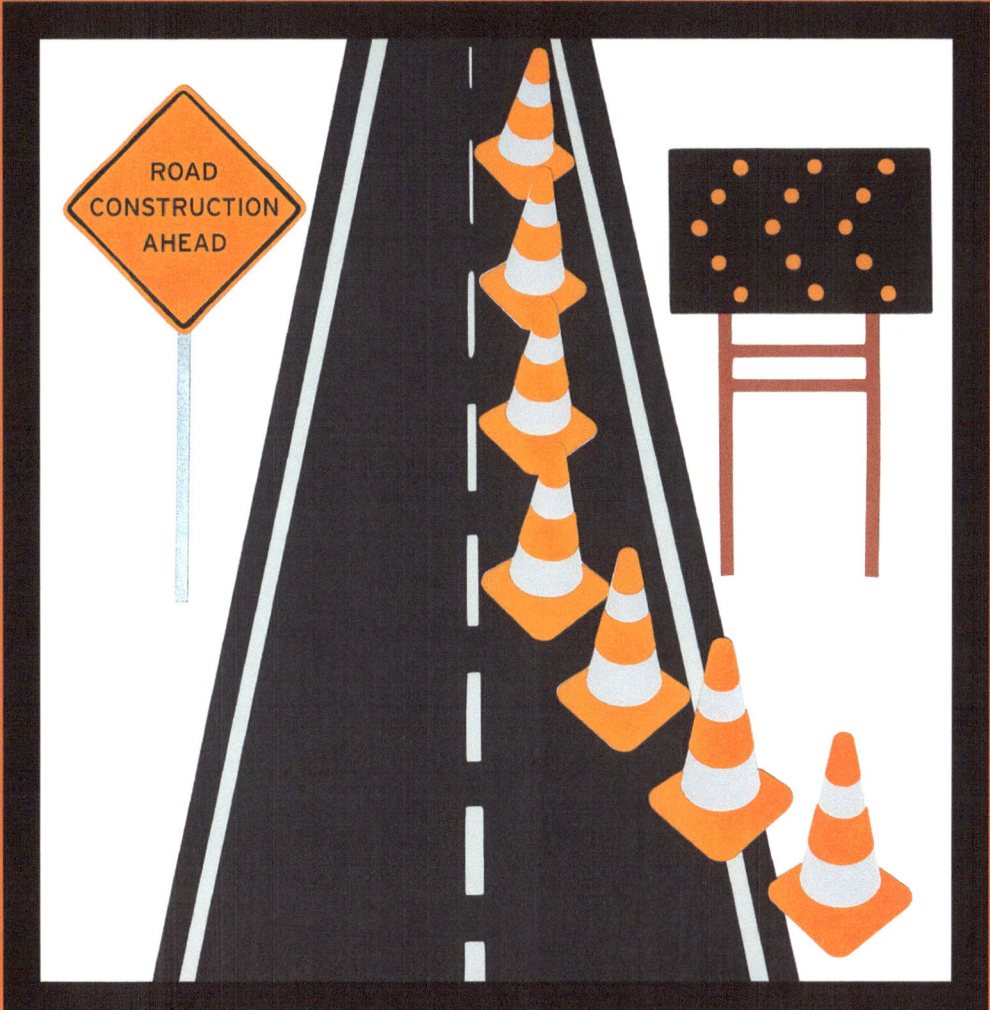

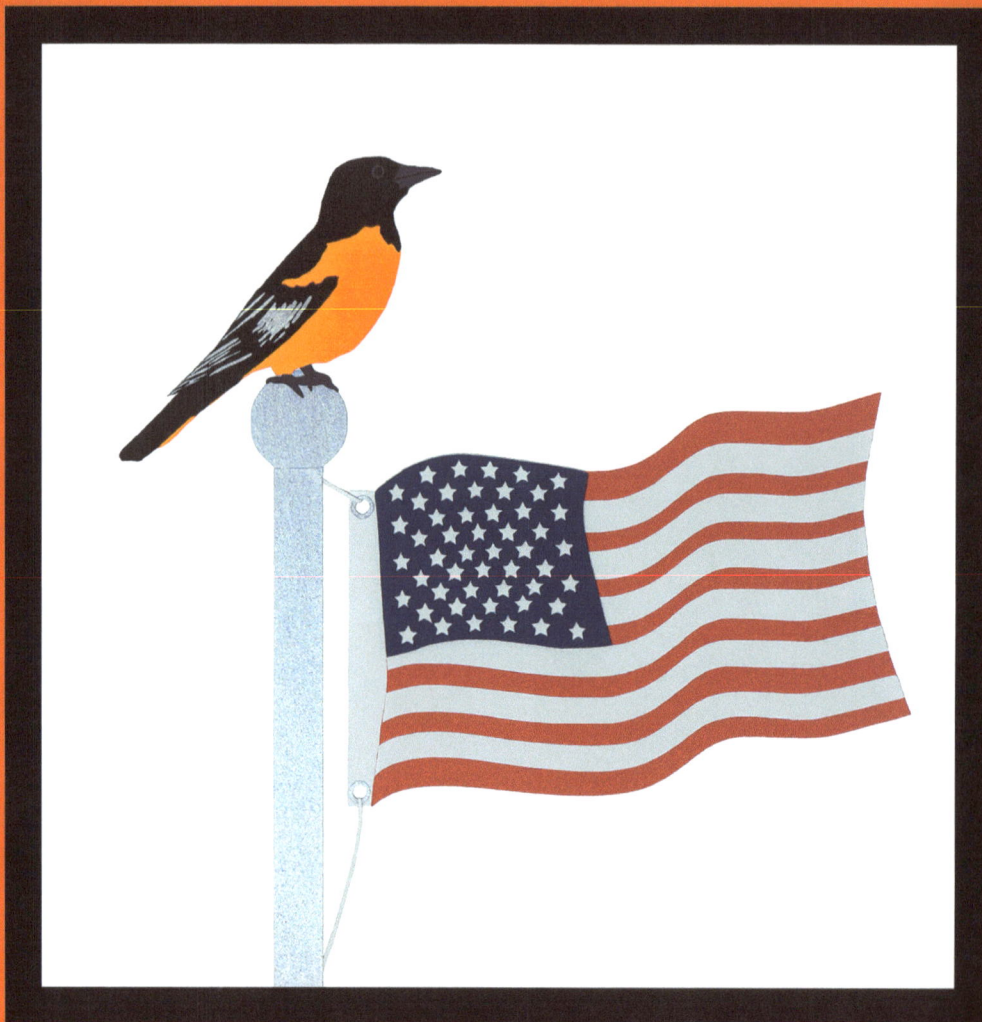

AND A BALTIMORE ORIOLE ON A FLAGPOLE!

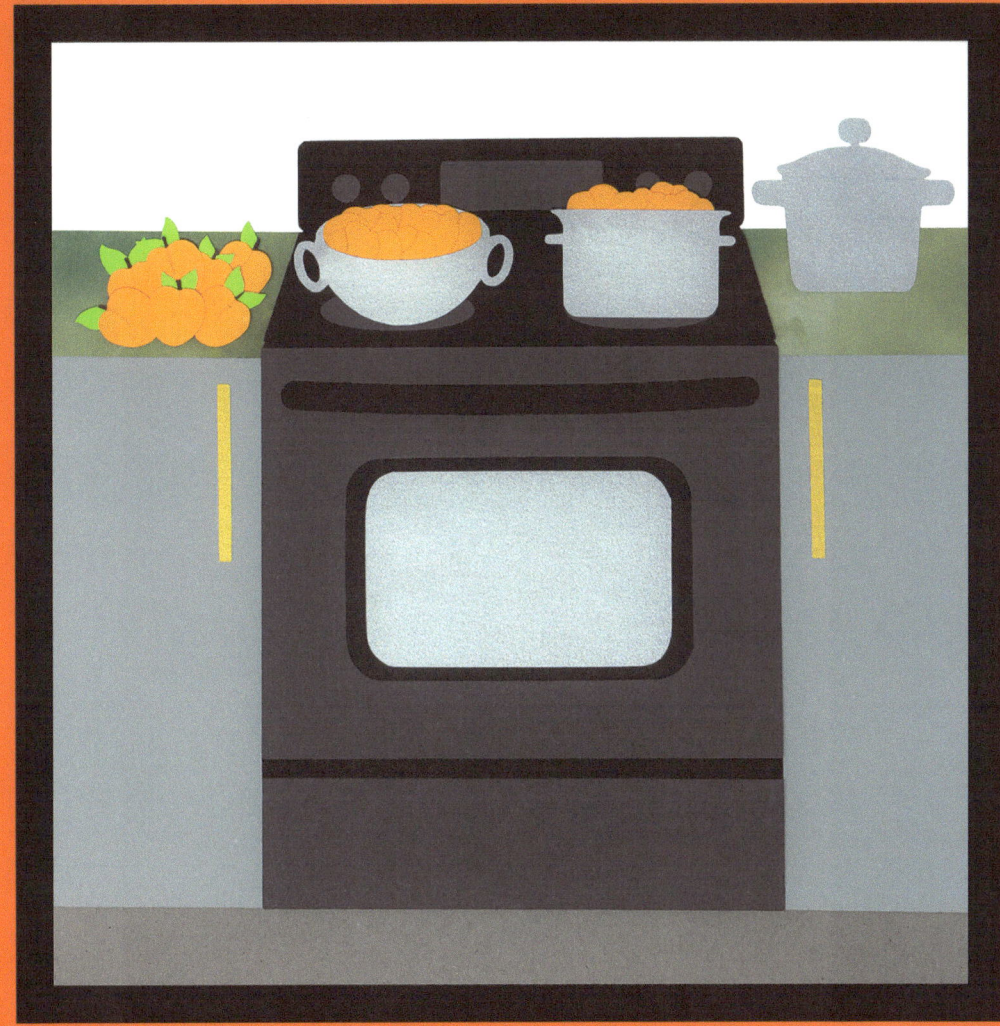

HERE ARE POTS OF APRICOTS...

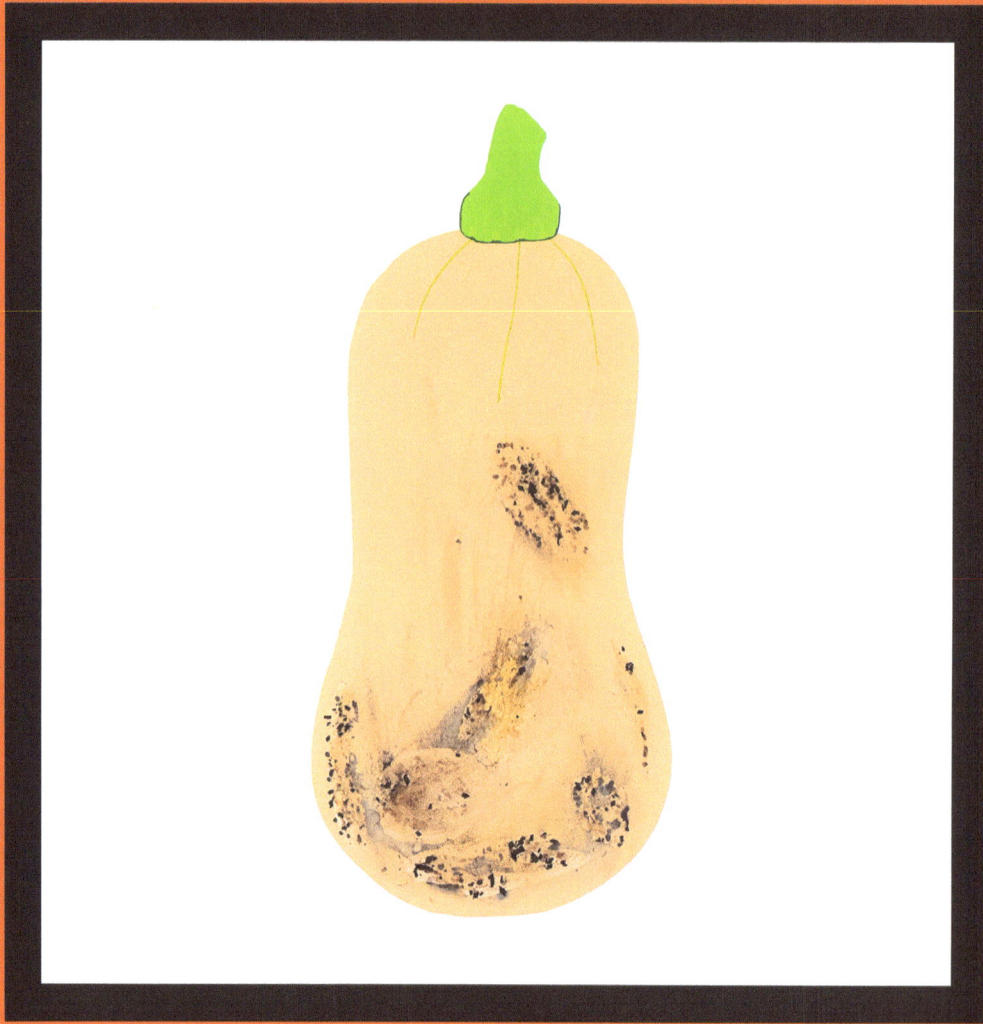

AND A BUTTERNUT SQUASH THAT NEEDS A WASH!

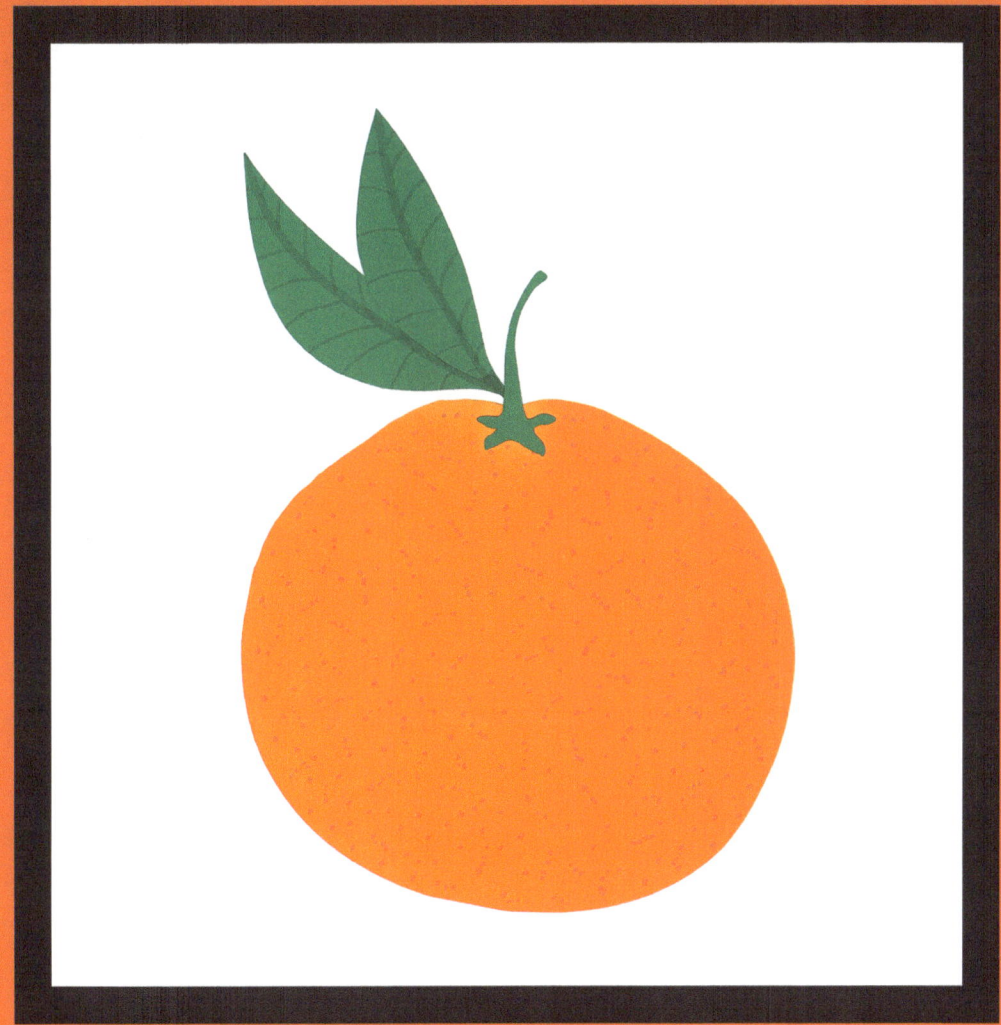

DID YOU KNOW THAT A CLEMENTINE IS THE SAME SIZE AS A LIME?

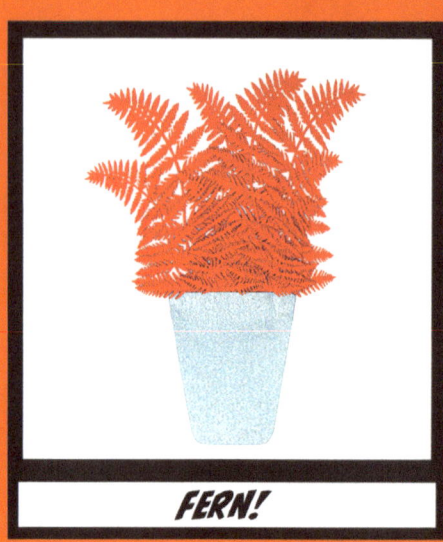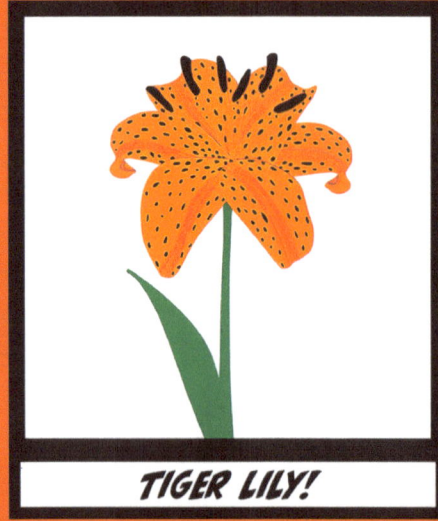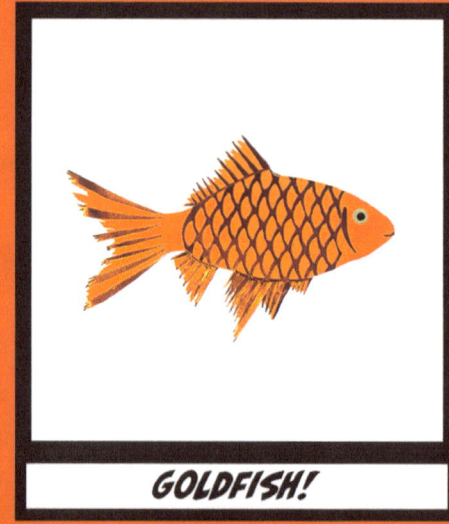

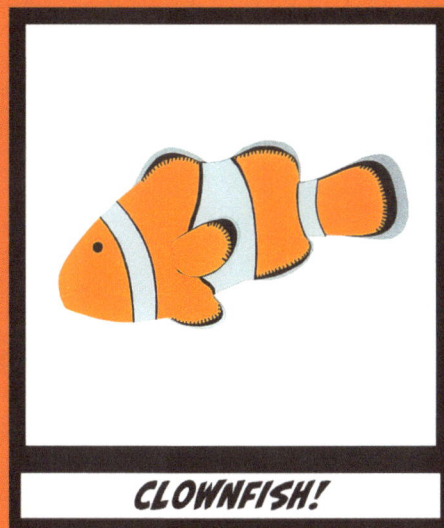

CLOWNFISH!

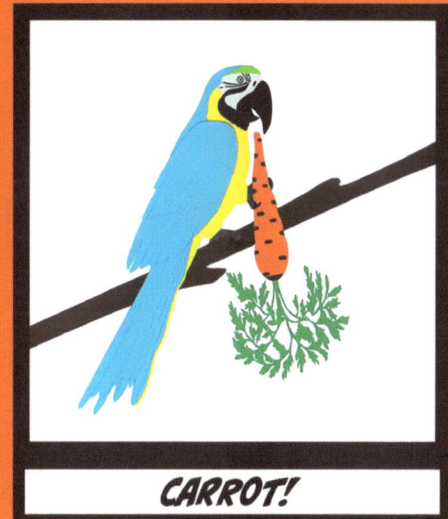

CARROT!

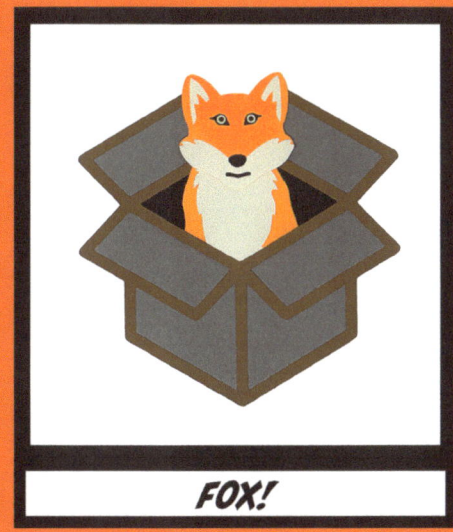

FOX!

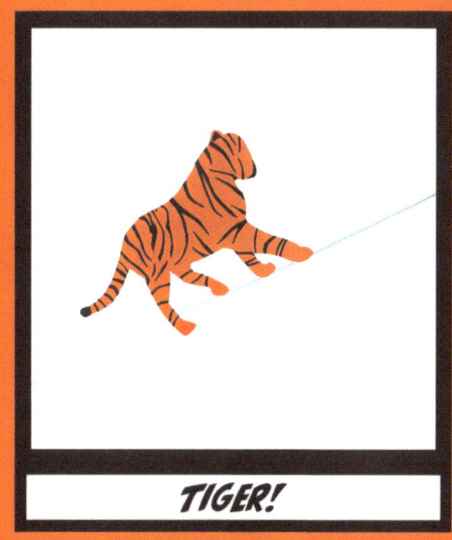

TIGER!

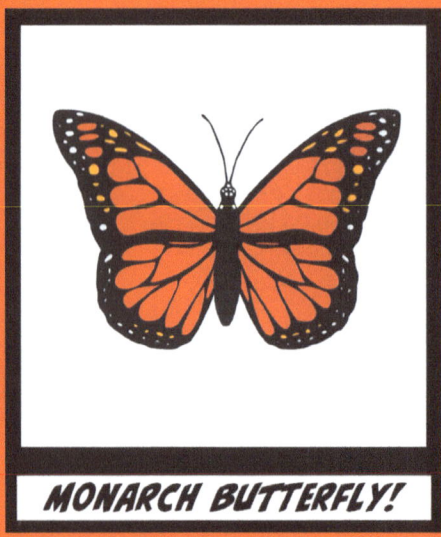
MONARCH BUTTERFLY!

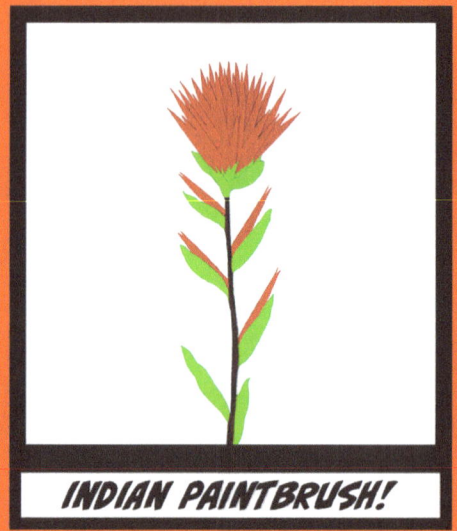
INDIAN PAINTBRUSH!

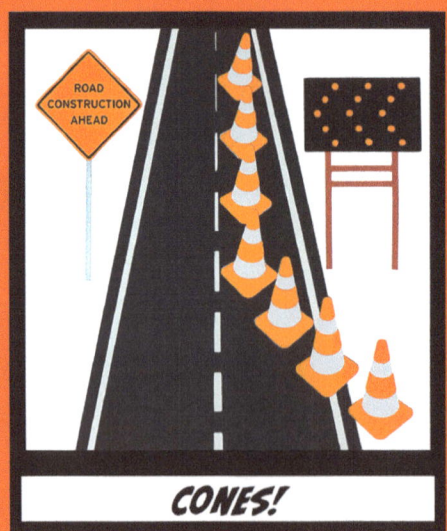
CONES!

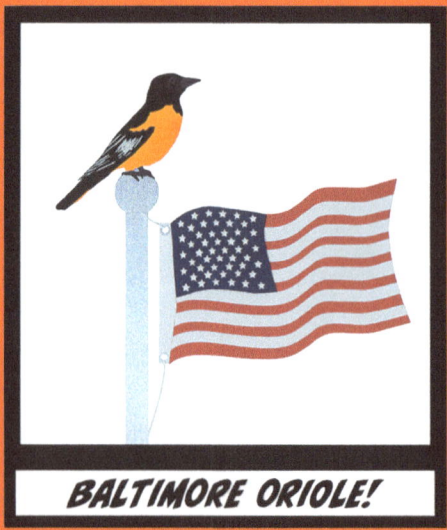
BALTIMORE ORIOLE!

APRICOTS!

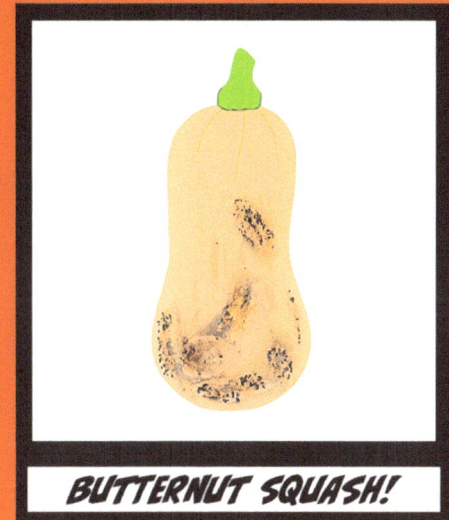
BUTTERNUT SQUASH!

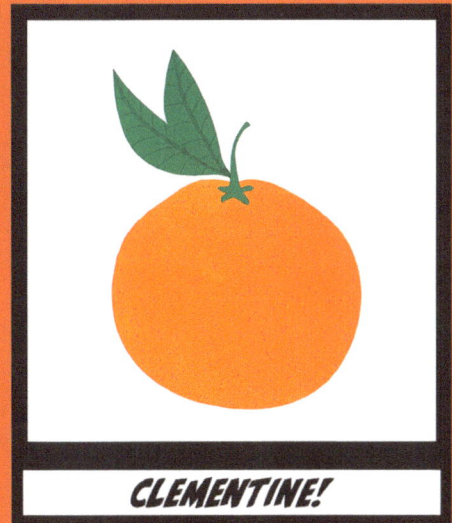
CLEMENTINE!

NICE JOB, AND NOW WE'RE THROUGH. ISN'T IT FUN TO LEARN SOMETHING NEW!

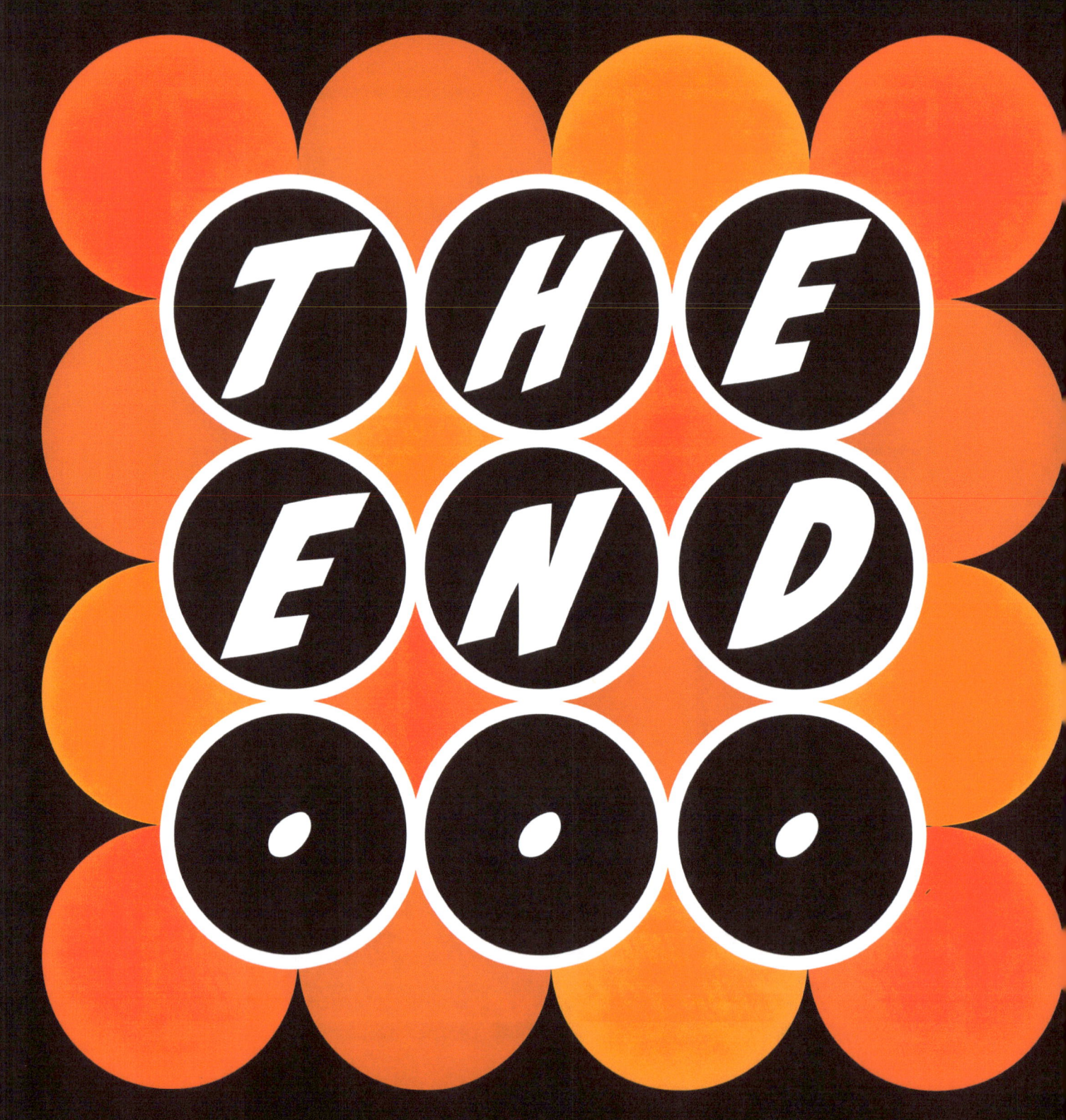

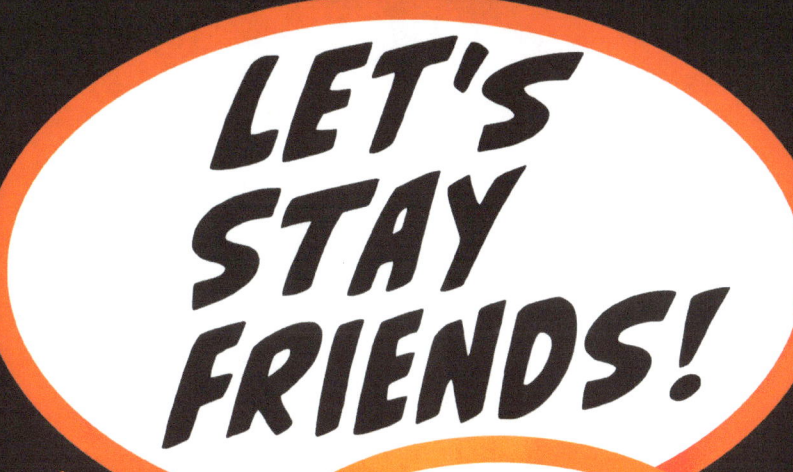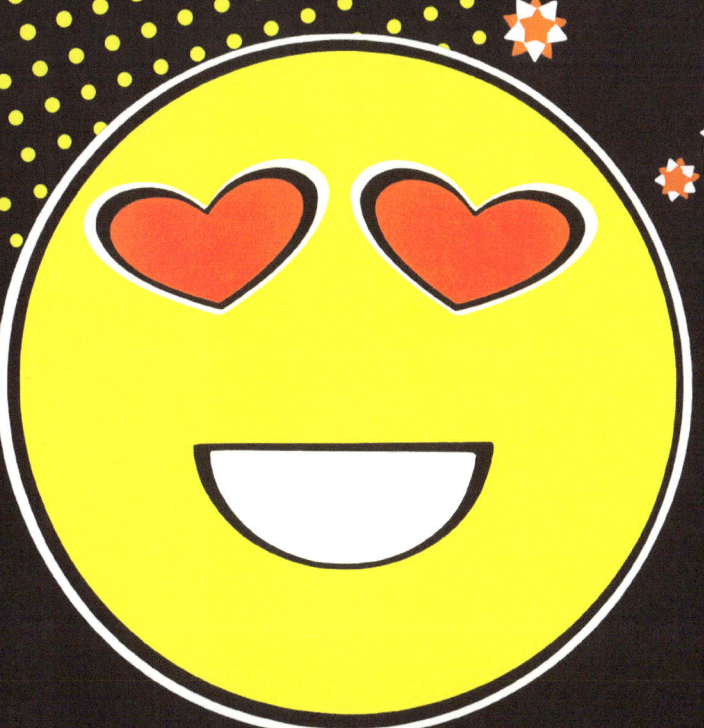

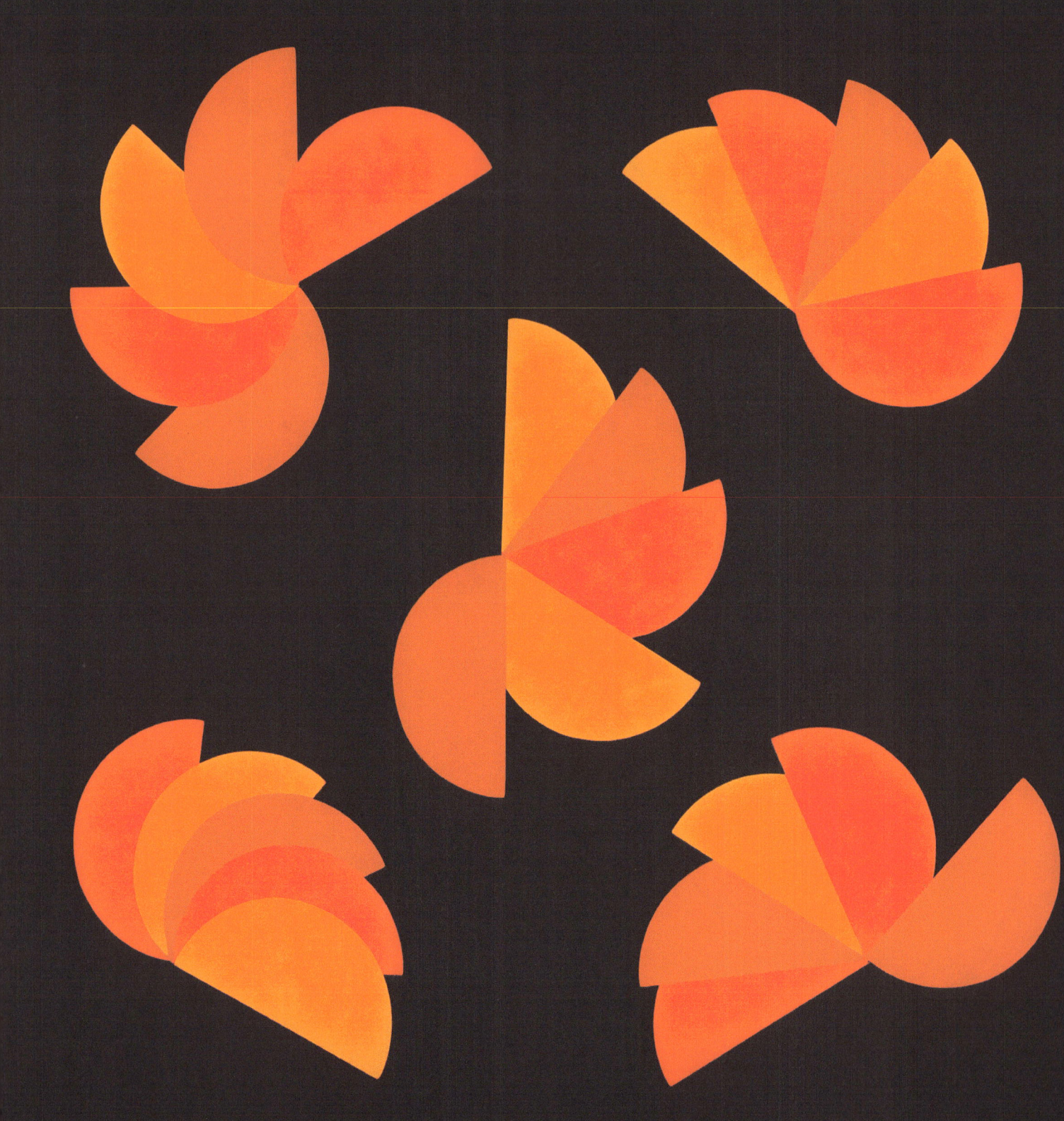

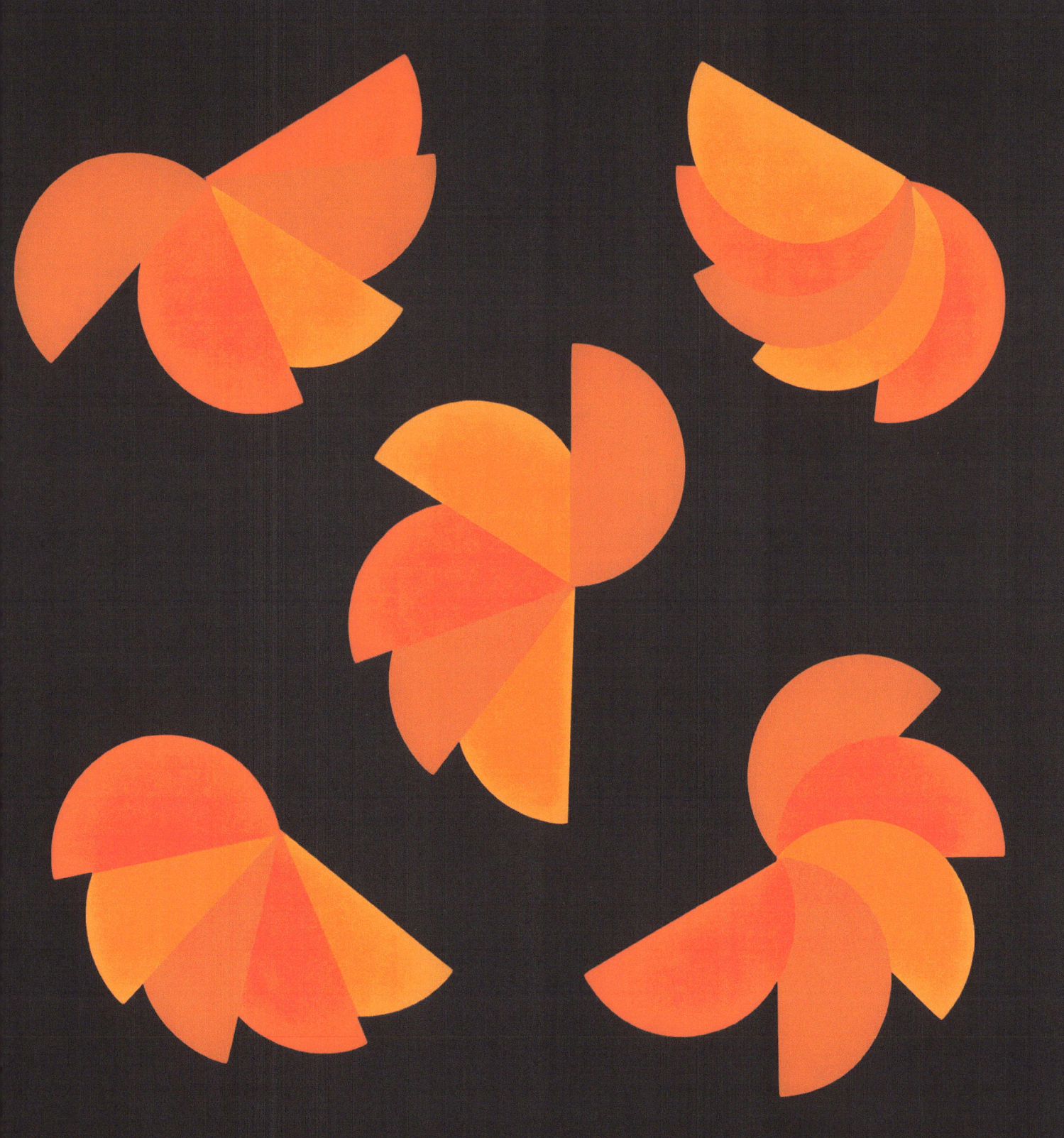

POP ART BOOKs AVAILABLE NOW

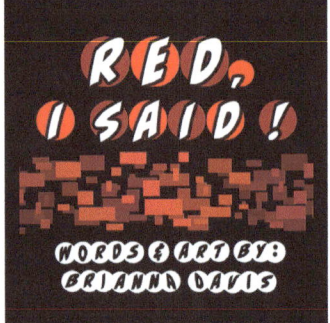
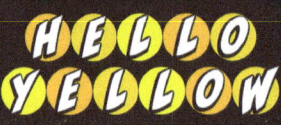
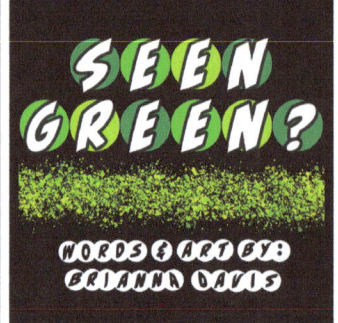
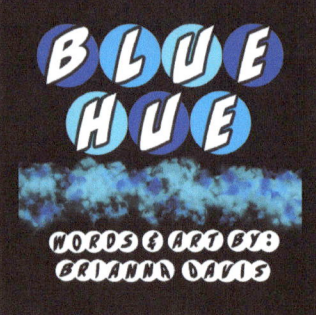
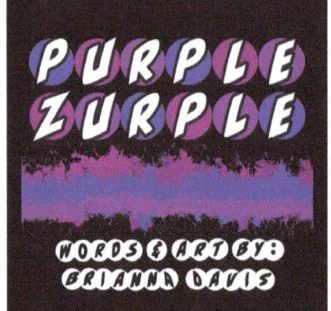
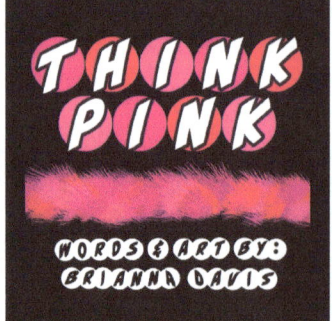
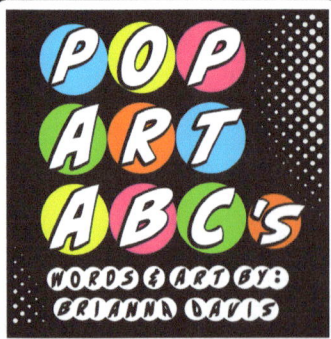
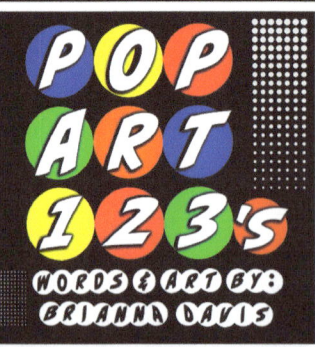

www.ingramcontent.com/pod-product-compliance
Lightning Source LLC
Chambersburg PA
CBHW051829210526
45473CB00005B/1799